Free Logic

Rachael Briggs was born in 1982 in Syracuse, New York and now lives in Brisbane. She holds a PhD in philosophy from the Massachusetts Institute of Technology, and splits her time between Griffith University and the Australian National University as a philosophy research fellow.

Her suite of sonnets 'Tough Luck' won the 2011 Val Vallis award for unpublished poetry. Her poems have also appeared in print (*Rattle, The Tower Journal*) and onstage (Speedpoets, Riverbend Poetry Series, Words or Whatever).

THE ARTS QUEENSLAND THOMAS SHAPCOTT POETRY PRIZE SERIES

Lidija Cvetkovic *War Is Not the Season for Figs*
Jaya Savige *Latecomers*
Nathan Shepherdson *Sweeping the Light Back Into the Mirror*
Angela Gardner *Parts of Speech*
Sarah Holland-Batt *Aria*
Felicity Plunkett *Vanishing Point*
Rosanna Licari *An Absence of Saints*
Vlanes *Another Babylon*
Nicholas Powell *Water Mirrors*

WINNER
OF THE
2012
THOMAS
SHAPCOTT
POETRY
PRIZE

Rachael Briggs
Free Logic

UQP

First published 2013 by University of Queensland Press
PO Box 6042, St Lucia, Queensland 4067 Australia

www.uqp.com.au
uqp@uqp.uq.edu.au

Design by Sandy Cull, gogoGingko
Typeset in 11.5/14 pt Adobe Garamond by Post Pre-press Group, Brisbane
Printed in Australia by McPherson's Printing Group

Queensland
Government
Arts Queensland

Sponsored by the Queensland Office
of Arts and Cultural Development

National Library of Australia Cataloguing-in-Publication entry
is available from the National Library of Australia http://catalogue.nla.gov.au/

ISBN 978 0 7022 4993 8 (pbk)
ISBN 978 0 7022 5189 4 (PDF)
ISBN 978 0 7022 5190 0 (ePub)
ISBN 978 0 7022 5191 7 (Kindle)

to my teachers

Contents

Twelve Love Stories
Ice   3
Slush   4
Mud   6
Biting Insects   7
Frogs   8
Smoke   9
Heat   10
Raspberries   11
Cider   12
Halloween   13
Frost   14
Snow   15

Solve for X and Y
Conversation Hearts   19
Ham   21
The Care and Feeding of Prehistoric Reptiles   23
Singularity   25
Flavours   26
Fatherhood   28
Minnow   29
Watchdog   31
Invisible   32
Swampy   34
Tits   35
Money for Nothing   37
Paint It Pink   39
Evening Wear   41

Tough Luck
King for an Evening   45
My Feet are Three Sizes Too Small   46
Wise Up   47
That Jackal   48
Thanks for Inviting Me   49
Your Cousin Lends Me His Shoes   50
The Party Ends   51

Deadly Sevenlings
Wrath   55
Lust   56
Gluttony   57
Envy   58
Sloth   59
Vanity   60
Avarice   61

Toothfish
Secret Sideshow   65
Their Burgeoning Friendship   66
Sabotage   67
He'll Be Back   68
Recovery   69
He's Sick of Being Back   70
Shipwreck   71
Epilogue   72

Cryptid Riddles
A Warning from the Park Ranger   75
Lonely Hearts Ad   76
College Life   77
How to Drop 12 Inches in 1 Week!   78

Dingo Complains About the Australian Music Scene   79
Mysterious Outback Figure   80
Banjo   81
Rough Times   82

This Poem is Not About You

Confessional   85
Romantic Comedies Give Me the Screaming Meemies   86
My Enemy   87
Bypass   88
Gnostic   89
Pushpin   90
The Kingdom of Ends Ain't All It's Cracked Up to Be   91

Logic Lectures

Eristic   95
Free Logic   96
Possible Dragons   97
Zeno's Paradoxes   98
Truth   100
The Phenomenal Paint Emporium   101
Waiting for David K. Lewis   103

Pointy Little Stones

Classic Rock   107
Burning   108
Sunbathers at the Gold Coast   109
Wooing Entropy   110
How Much is Not Enough?   111
Third Gender Roles   112

Notes   113
Acknowledgements   117

Twelve Love Stories

Ice

When the cosmic glassmaker blasts his blowtorch
over trees and trash cans, anneals the snow banks,
seals the pickerel under a frosted panel,
that's when I need you.

Melt for me. Glow gold where the chips of sunlight
tangle through your hair. We can meld our colours.
Twist me, trail your tongue through my mouth, and we'll be
red reticello.

Soon I'll leave. The snowmelt will scour the river,
swell the lake and shatter the ice. We're spun from
inconsistent glass. In the heat, we'll crackle,
crumble to gravel.

but today, my love is as sharp as pikes' teeth,
naked as the glass in a hungry pike's eye.

Slush

Hand in hand, we struggle toward the Red Line.
What if I froze feet-first against the sidewalk?
You'd wade back in your beard and pink galoshes,
ready to save me.

Great. My toes are numb, but I feel the blizzard
inching up my ankles. Thank God—here's Kendall.
Someday when we're rich, we can buy a chopper,
soar through the snowstorms.

On the platform, teenagers clump and whisper.
With luck, they'll ignore us. No, now they're pointing.
Shit. We should've taken a cab. They'll bash us
to queer smithereens.

Here they come. One smirks, 'Is it male or female?'
You return his gaze. 'Maybe not.' I wonder
idly whether the cops will find our bodies
covered in knife wounds,

but the train clanks in, so I tug your coat sleeve,
drag you through the steel double doors. He spits back
some retort and turns to his friends. They're laughing,
slapping his shoulders.

Home and warm, my chest full of slush, I clutch you.
Wish I'd borne you up like a god of mercy.
Wish I'd smashed his face like an angry angel.
Maybe I'm neither.

Mud

Thick as Karo syrup, it climbs our pant legs,
snogs us shoe to shinbone. The collie loves it,
snorts it with her steam shovel nose, rolls over,
happy tongue lolling.

When we dreamt of spring, our tongues ached for peaches.
Plums, we whispered. *Gooseberries. Bright red rhubarb.*
Bring me zephyrs warm with the smell of bath salts:
tulip and lilac.

What we got was mud. Clods of clay and humus
lodge between our toes and our swollen gym socks.
Now the dog needs bathing. Our jeans need scouring;
they're grey as rainclouds.

Come indoors. We'll soak in the tub of winter.
I'll fetch the bath salts.

Biting Insects

Mark but this flea, and mark in this,
How little that which thou deniest me is
     – John Donne

Biting flies are back. Let our bloods be mingled.
If your beard veers whitish, if I'm no maiden,
still we burst with juices. The wanton blackflies
sup on our ripeness.

They return each year; our welts rise to meet them.
Berry-mad, we grasp them between our fingers,
crush the bloated lobes til our palms turn purple,
taste the raw tingle.

How the forest buzzes with black abundance!
From old bottles, gutters, the mouths of tires,
life zooms forth, the mirrors of scum reflecting
perfect imagoes.

If this fly be marriage bed, marriage temple,
marry me again. Let us be remade.

Frogs

Kid, I never ordered a baby brother.
I said *chicken nuggets*. Oh well. The kitchen
won't replace you now that you've dipped your fingers
into the creek muck.

Grab that stick and follow. Let's make the best of
all the forts. We'll stuff it with frogs and Mars bars,
dinosaurs and eggs and green soldiers. You can
act as my sidekick.

First step: tadpoles. Hand me that bucket. Climb up
on that slippery rock, and we'll scare them in.
When they change to bullfrogs, all brown and bulgy,
I'll give you half.

Smoke

He was *bad*: he crashed up his father's outboard,
smoked his mother's Camels behind the outhouse,
snuck out late, bought beer off his older brother,
souped up his beater.

We were *thick*: I wove you a rainbow bracelet,
spun you colt's-foot garlands. We huddled barefoot,
sliced our thumbs and blended our blood like sisters,
closer than lovers

'til he gunned his truck past your father's cabin.
Lit your heart. The heat of the gas combustion
charred me like a marshmallow. I was ashwood
stricken to ashes.

You were *gone*. Sped off in his phoney hot rod.
I lit up the charcoal grill, gnawed a hot dog
by myself. I crouched in a haze of mesquite,
crushing mosquitoes.

Heat

Warm with rum, we snuck out to catch the sunset
in our teeth. You whispered, 'I'll fuck your brains out.'
So much pumping and sweat, but you're not done yet.
Come, kiss me deeper.

Half my neck is purple; it's only bruises.
Bite me harder, beat me; you'll never break this
hunger. Bend me over the stove; I'm burning
all my illusions.

Go on, crush me; cover my mouth. I'll scratch you.
Let me wrap your scapula up in scrimshaw.
Be my tusk and I'll be your blade. I'll scribble
tangible poems

on your skin. Are you food enough to fill me?
You're as salty as olives. I'm so hungry.

Raspberries

I know only one cure for chronic August:
picking raspberries. Paint your palate scarlet.
True, the thorns will embroider matching ribbons
over your ankles,

but the liquor will only trickle faster
through your throat to the veins that sting and whisper,
thirsty, thirsty. Go, saunter through the brambles.
Open your body.

I stood stark in a thicket, picking berries
for my lover. A treble leaf betrayed me.
Berries bloomed on my skin for weeks, like itching
pastoral etchings.

When my lover betrayed me too, I wondered:
where's the beauty in brambles now? I ate, then,
all the berries I'd picked for her. The juices
dripped down my fingers.

Cider

Once I loved a sapling. He smacked of sunshine,
kissed me wet and tart as a Cortland apple,
filled my arms with flowers. The bees grew hazy,
dizzy with pollen.

Fall and fall, his shadow spread broad, fermenting
Jonagold and Empire. I knitted lichen
shawls to warm his shoulders. The bees brewed honey
dark as molasses.

Now I tipple cider spiked sharp with nutmeg.
(That, and brandy. Keeps off the frost.) Arthritis
knots my knuckles hard, but the bees drink hardy
under our seedlings.

When his trunk groans hollow, I'll bear his branches
on an oaken prop. I will mulch my orchard
'til the east wind ices the beehive empty,
echoes my tombstone.

Halloween

Let's gulp syrup under the sugar maples.
Grab your gumballs, candy corn, wax lips, chocolate
kisses. Grip your pillowcase by the edges;
rip it asunder.

Glory in the flurry of candy apples.
Grin while gelt hails down in a rainbow torrent:
jelly babies, jawbreakers bright as budgies,
whirlybird splendour.

Chomp those beauties. Gorge til the street lamp stipples
sticky lips and stomachs. Slurp cherry sunset.
Let the leaves flame down; let the evening hedges
blaze out like tinder.

Frost

Past the Old Crown Mill, past the oaks, we hustle,
chop the trail to eight-minute miles, dip back
down the gorge to cut through the grizzled graveyard,
me and my father.

Blunt cleats claw me onward, but he'll outpace me
on the uphill stretch to Thanksgiving dinner.
Borne on Boston Marathon legs, he'll leave me
cold in his contrail.

Every year, he wins. Every year, I'm gaining.
Hoarfrost salts the grass, and his hair shines silver.
This sharp wind that chisels my calves and hamstrings
whittles him thinner.

Soon, November's hawk will uncurl its talons,
dash a daughter's heart on the frosty drumlins.

Snow

Me in sweatpants, you in midmorning whiskers,
planning out the last of our winter weekend.
Yesterday: bad sci fi and Islay whisky.
Now: I need coffee.

God, it's cold. Last night, it snowed fifteen inches.
Let's stay in and chill. I'll enjoy this instant
Folgers shit. Go on, make it bitter, inky.
Rust out my innards.

Burn me like your idiot friend who called me
'frigid bitch' and asked if you'd ever nailed me.
Yeah, he asked me out. You were right; he wants me.
Wish I had talons.

There's the phone. You answer. I hear your mother
whirring like a blender. You blush and stammer.
When you waste your weekends on me, you murder
possible children.

Guess we're trapped; the snow shows no sign of calming.
Every flake is bright as a tiny comet.
Hanging up, you smile. 'Shall we read some comics?
Good day for Iceman.'

Snowdrifts build. Remember the time I kissed you
years ago? We paused in the sunlit kitchen,
sugar-specked, the tips of our tastebuds catching
marzipan sweetness.

Solve for X and Y

Conversation Hearts

Dolores puked birthday frosting all over
her fairy godmother's suede pumps.
The old woman stiffened
beneath her lace collar.
Too prim to curse in front of the children,
she hissed an enchantment
in the umbra of her bedside lampshade.

Instead of questions, witticisms, or transcendental arguments,
Dolores hacked up chalky candies
engraved with dye.

WHATEVER
U WANT

CUTE SHOES
NICE WEATHER

I DON T
GET
POLITICS

SORRY
THE HOUSE
IS A MESS

SUCH
A PRETTY
PRINCESS

I DON T MIND
REALLY
IT'S OK

When she turned 30
her throat ran out of Red #40
so she spat wafers
into the potted cactus
until even the sugar dwindled.
Her words shrunk to birdseed,
pinheads.

Finally, she coughed up a hunk of quartzite
that said
NO in sharp letters.

It tasted clean.

Ham

Ike designed an antenna
to pick up longwave radio from other worlds.
Hello, crackled the speaker,
This is Ike.
I've been living on brie and strawberries
since I won the Nobel Prize
for inventing the trans-world transmitter.

The multiverse was full of them:
inventor Ikes, Ikes in heavy metal bands, biker Ikes,
welder, pilot, stockbroker, and dancer Ikes,
dragonback Ikes who played fire polo,
down-and-out Ikes, jailbird Ikes,
Ikes who ditched their wives for a young heiress,
slave-owning Ikes.
'I would never do that,' said Ike.
You don't understand the historical context,
they hissed. *Anyway, we* are *you.*

The antenna had one engineering flaw:
no off switch.
Ike the Failure tuned in at three every morning.
I tried to kill myself, but I couldn't turn the oven on.
Thank God you're so close—
just a pink slip between you and me.
During awkward family conversations,
Ike the Guilt Trip would pop onto the airwaves.
Why are you so needy?
I let my relatives eat my liver once

so that nobody had to go hungry.
It grew back.

Worst of all was Ike Who Is Better Than Ike.
I got engaged.
People say twenty-five is a little young,
but we both know what we want.
Besides, we can afford a nice honeymoon
since my private practice is thriving
and her modelling career has taken off.
Ike hurled the antenna into the bathtub
but only gave himself a nasty shock.

The *New Scientist* ran an article
about advances in communication technology.
Ike has no comment;
he's working on a pair of earplugs.

The Care and Feeding of Prehistoric Reptiles

Denise was born with a small pterodactyl
lodged in her gut. *It's perfectly normal,*
the doctor told her parents.

But in the middle of gym class,
it gouged her with its egg tooth.
Denise was sent to the nurse,
who gave her an aspirin, a new pair of shorts,
and a pamphlet.

Your dinosaur is precious.
Wash it daily.
Never touch it.
Keep it clean and pure
for your future husband and children.

Every month, the pterodactyl squirmed, bit,
spat out blood.
Denise's nightmares grew gravid:
fat green cantaloupes
pulsed with half-formed life.
She took anti-reptile pills,
cooked omelettes and frittatas.
The biting abated a little.

When, thirty-five years later,
the animal died in a flailing fit,
Denise made an appointment to have it removed.
The young doctor suggested couples counselling

with her husband
to help them grieve.
Her partner Gertrude
laughed about this for weeks.

Singularity

Stuart glued electrodes to his scalp
in preparation for the Great Upload.
He crammed his hard drive
full of blueprints for a cyborg city:
turbines, turrets, turbo tanks.

When the slime moulds took over,
they soaked his laptop in digestive goo.
You're being emotional! he shrieked
as a plasmoid slithered up his torso
into his ear.
He tried to scream again
in Esperanto
but the fruiting bodies had by this time
occluded his airway,
and it was becoming difficult
to think.

Flavours

Justine rocked up to the Fetish Flea
fifteen minutes early
lugging a gigantic leather tote.
To carry my new fetish home, she explained.
I'm not sure what it will be,
but it may require heavy machinery.

A man in clover clamps
suggested flogging.
Great learning curve. You can practise at home
with a squash racket or a wooden spoon.
One end stung and the other wore her arm to wobbly string.

She persuaded a leather daddy to trim her with rope.
He slithered it across her breasts, back, thighs
until she towered on a puff of hempen air, a postmodern sculpture
that badly needed to pee.
Thank God for safety shears, he said.

When she worried her tongue over a spike-heeled pump,
she only tasted feet.
Lace tickled, latex chafed, and leather smelled of dead horses.
Strawberry lube
had nothing to do with strawberries.
In the back room,
she fainted at the sight of needles.
The electricity smelled like burning.

She slunk home at midnight
peppered with cane marks and wax welts,
still dragging that empty bag.
Her boyfriend didn't ask,
just poured two mugs of Sleepytime Vanilla.
Later, in the queen-sized feather bed,
they fell asleep kissing.

Fatherhood

Joshua's wife gave birth to a tiger cub.
She had trouble coping with the implications
and took up with the dogcatcher,
leaving Joshua to care for Maddy.

He hardly minded. Dizzy
over his daughter's olive eyes and savannah smell,
he strolled her through the state park
singing campfire songs.

When friends suggested a paternity test,
he blew raspberries in their faces.
'That's tiger puke on my shirt,' he pointed out.
'Of course I'm her dad.'

He enrolled her in a special cat preschool.
Lionesses gave them the flehmen face
and speculated on whether an apeman
could grasp the nuances of mince and litter,

but he coached Maddy with flashcards,
packed half a chicken into her lunchbox every evening,
sanded the claw marks off the furniture,
watched her stretch and bulge into a tigress.

She's climbing mountains now, in Nepal,
but she visits at Christmas.
She puts away the whole turkey
and lets her old man win at arm wrestling.

Minnow

Simone, always terrified of fish,
caught a pink minnow
in the deadfall of her stomach.
It nibbled the twigs of her capillaries,
but finding them bitter, yipped for a banana sandwich,
which it hurled back up her throat.

To fling it out to sea,
said the doctor,
would require either a completed parental notification form
    or a judicial bypass, in addition to an ultrasound and two
    counselling sessions with a clinically-trained psychologist.
Simone wished his toupee would melt off his head.

She fed the minnow Coke and Pop Rocks,
jerked it through five hundred jumping jacks,
dragged it to see *Saw II* playing in theatres,
and punched it in the stomach,
but each morning, it failed to appear belly-up in the toilet bowl.

Instead, it flipped and stretched,
grew stubby legs and a beaver belly,
keened for mud cake to build a fat lodge 'round Simone's navel.
How could you? wailed her mother,
but she didn't throw Simone out.

When it reached the size of a largemouth bass,
the minnow swam for land,
slicing Simone
with its fin, thin as the one
Simone had drawn through her mother.

Watchdog

Whenever Tyrone edged onto a sidewalk,
polite white ladies
shimmered away.

A terror in pinstripes,
an alligator in Italian oxblood shoes,
he soaked the street in his shadow.
Though he signed his name T. Anthony Washington,
respectable people backed away, smiling
with tiny cold teeth.
Not even daisies would look him in the eye.

He bought a dog to protect himself
from other people's fear.
Mitzi has to leap to lick strangers' knees,
but Tyrone is taller now.
He's teaching her agility
and the science of fetching a stick.
People pause to admire her feathered ears.
On cool evenings, she curls on the couch
in the warmth of Tyrone's shadow.

Invisible

When Zola bought a black cauldron at a garage sale
the old woman chucked in the cookbook for free.
Now it falls open to page 13, where
if you squint through the moiré of ancient sauces
you can nearly make out
Cloak of Invisibility with Truffle Oil.
(Zola substitutes butter and button mushrooms.)

The stuff knocks the whorls out of your ears,
blasts your eyebrows bushy,
puts hair on your upper lip—
but that's the point.
Last week, Zola sashayed through the centre of town
in hot pants.
As she waggled her mushroom-fed ass,
people bit their lips and looked away.

'Hello handsome,'
she breathed into the ear of a blond bricklayer.
He gazed deep into his wall.
'I've got two tickets to *Cirque du Soleil*.'
His eyes didn't even swerve.

Every Sunday, she simmers a picnic stew in the cauldron
for her cat Fabrizio
and her invisible friends Heather and Wendy.

Shy luna moths, broad as belt buckles,
perch on their hats.
White-throated sparrows trill from the trellis
(I see nobody nobody nobody)
as the ladle lifts itself.

Swampy

Brayden was sick of being a fag
so he gained fifteen kilos of protein shake
and bought a pair of winkle-pickers.
He stomped around with a throat full of Fourex,
Beasts of Bourbon pouring through his ears.
Nobody fucked with him.

He got a job at the abattoir,
which covered rent, shrooms, and groceries,
but there was no one to talk politics with,
and his creepy colleague stared at him
while drawing a knife across the cows' throats.

So Brayden moved to Fortitude Valley,
Brisneyland,
and opened a book store.
He sits behind the counter and reads his fag books:
Jane Austen, George Eliot, the Bröntes.
Nobody fucks with him.

Tits

When Miranda stands before God—
not that she believes in a God,
not that she'd give Him the satisfaction—

but if there were a day of reckoning
she'd slap that almighty bastard across His omnimalevolent face
for pinning them to her chest
like some prank sign.

Squeeze the melons.
Pet the sweater puppies.
Bounce the beach balls.
Man the torpedoes.
Dairy fun bags: all you can grab!

She's not stupid;
she got the joke by the time she was fourteen.
Whenever she slouched through the mall
or hunched in the corner of the bus stop bench,
invisible ink would appear, miraculously
reflected in the eyes of grown men
who eyed her naked body
through two baggy tee-shirts and a sports bra.

Get a load of them
bazoombas, kawangas, maguppies, palookas,
dingleboppers, chumbawumbas, jellybonkers, windshield wipers,
jugs, cans, baps, norks,

mammaries, cantaloupes, bibelots, chesticles,
hooters, whimwhams, yazoos, cha-chas,
teetees, tatas, wapbopaloobops
BOOBS!

You can't wash that off.

But in the steam of her early-morning shower,
Miranda blushes like sunrise.
Holding one in each hand,
she strokes them as softly
as you'd stroke a pair of floppy bunnies.
Since the right one is the tiniest splash fuller,
she cranes her neck down and lifts it to her lips
for a kiss.
'Mine,' she growls,
in case anyone is paying attention.

She knows that omniscient prick is watching her
(if He even exists)
cursing His transcendental lack of hands.
She hopes He's jealous.

Money for Nothing

Denny found a coupon in the back of *Guitar World*
that entitled him to one (1) girlfriend.
He enclosed five dollars
and a note:
prefer blonde, round buttocks, fond of drum kits, thank you.

A golden-haired UPS woman rang his doorbell,
apologised for the wrong address,
and left.
The mail carrier brought
a tax document
and a flyer from the pizza parlour.
They probably used the seven-day shipping option,
he told his Ginger Reyes poster.
She'll get here.

When it became evident
that the mailbox held only bills and junk mail,
he stepped up his game,
scouring clubs for clues of her presence,
slipping his number to record store clerks,
feeding pick-up lines to babes on the street.

They rejected him.
He brought letters of recommendation from his scoutmaster
and offered to buy dinner.
No dice.
He went home and stroked himself to Ginger Reyes,
gorged himself on Doritos
until his heart turned into a Mars bar
and he ate it.

Paint It Pink

Lauren's sister said *if your head wasn't full of marshmallow fluff*
you wouldn't waste your time on ruffles and lipstick.
Lauren buckled her skates,
grabbed a roller
and a bottomless bucket of paint.

She rumbled through the university labs,
coating laser, microtome, cyclotron, electron microscope
in a fandango film.
Men of science in Baker-Miller lab coats
whipped off their rose-coated glasses to squint
at the sequinned comet
splashing down the hallway.

The auto body shop was next:
rivet, ratchet, fan belt, muffler transfigured
from grease monkey grey to razzle dazzle rose;
all those mechanics shaking their heads
at the rocket girl who caromed fender to bumper, yelling,
I got wheels!

She coasted through the skate park, the US naval base,
the camouflage aisle at Toys R Us,
football fields, bistros, even the Catholic cathedral
where the priest
fainted flat into his communion wine.

When she wobbled to a stop
between a fuchsia letterbox and a magenta lamppost,
pink meant everything and nothing.
So pulling an olive green lipstick out of one pocket
and a compass out of the other,
she sailed home,
calculating tangents in her head.

Evening Wear

Lars felt the tie contract around his neck.
The zipper nipped. The jacket tensed its shoulders.
'Before a cufflink stabs me in the back,'
he said, 'I'd better split my seams.' He shuddered
his shirtsleeves off, undid his belt, unclicked
his watch. Hot wool fell slack, cold silver skittered

across the tiles, and, down to briefs,
Lars blinked: 'What's next? I'm underdressed
in smile and birthday suit.' He reached
past check and herringbone, to clasp,
at closet's end, a floral sheath,
and slipped into that silk at last.

Uncuffed, uncollared, clean:
freedom makes the man.

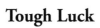

Tough Luck

King for an Evening

You think that I'm good-looking for a girl;
I'll take it over 'competent' or 'smart'.
(I nick my upper lip. That's going to smart
when I apply the spirit gum.) A girl
had better take what she can get. (I twist
the bandages around my chest—too tight—
can't breathe—unwrap and start again.) The tight-
rope thrill of you's enough. I guess the twist
(and twist and fasten) is the way my body
is less 'jewelled evening gown' than 'undershirt'.
No wonder you don't want it. (Undershirt
then button-up, then tie.) Would anybody?
(A dab of Old Spice. Hair gel, comb, slick back.
I check the mirror. Half a man looks back.)

My Feet are Three Sizes Too Small

I check the mirror. Half a man looks back,
his brow a smudge, his pointed chin a chime
of Dad's. My voice may be a reedy chime,
but how I love my beard and breadth of back!
If Dad were here, I wonder, would he call
me son and shake my hand? I wrap my tie
around my neck and think of how to tie
a Windsor knot, but somehow can't recall.
I think, instead, of Sundays as a girl:
brisk walks with Dad, slow brunches after Mass.
Behind the mirror, sunk inside a massive
dress-up suit, I glimpse a small, plain girl.
She cracks her knuckles, acting butch, but then,
she's crying in the bathroom yet again.

Wise Up

You're crying in the bathroom yet again.
I pass the tissues. Your mascara lies
in sodden clumps. 'Bold', 'waterproof'—all lies;
please swear you'll never touch the stuff again.
Please stop. Please make the crying stop. Please make
him hurt. I hate his hair, his skintight pants,
his Calvin Klein cologne, the lust he pants
all over you. It's not the clothes that make
me ill; I only wish you hadn't drunk
his vows like sparkling wine. I can't believe
at nearly thirty-three, you still believe
the utter shit men tell you when they're drunk.
If his martini gags him, who'll be sorry?
His smarm will melt in hell. I hope he's sorry.

That Jackal

His smarm will melt in hell, I hope. He's sorry
you were offended, but he didn't mean
to come across as cruel, he says; it's mean
to treat him like some criminal. The sorry
bouquet he's bought you exhales its perfume
(carnations in a puff of baby's breath)
straight in my face. I'll bet it takes your breath
away. I'm sure he'll buy you cheap perfume
and half-priced chocolates. Will they make you smile?
He stares at me, blinks eloquent appeal
from spaniel eyes. I squint. What's the appeal?
The fancy leather coat? The coydog smile?
I wonder what he keeps behind his teeth.
A razor blade? Another row of teeth?

Thanks for Inviting Me

A razor blade, another row of teeth—
these parties make me long for something sharp.
I'd never touch your cousins, but my sharp
new dress? Oh yeah, right in the whalebone teeth.
Don't get me wrong; I'm glad to be your date—
I see. Okay, whatever then. Your friend.
I'm proud of you. That boy was not your friend.
I simply can't choke down this sticky date
and saffron pudding, waltz in these high heels,
or comment on the wine's unique bouquet.
Good God, what now? They're tossing the bouquet?
You go; I'll sit and rub my aching heels.
These shoes crunch up my arches, so I drag
my feet. It makes me feel like I'm in drag.

Your Cousin Lends Me His Shoes

My feet! It makes me feel like I'm in drag
to rock these wicked wingtips. I could dance
a magic foxtrot, float above the dance
floor laughing, snog the cirrus clouds, and drag
the DJ with me. So I do. I step
out past the knots of uncles clutching glasses,
the clumps of aunts in scarves and cat-eye glasses,
into the centre of the floor. I step
the Charleston, moonwalk, grapevine, twist, bees' knees,
and tightrope. Hell, I even yell out 'Stop!'
and 'Hammertime!', but really, I won't stop
'til I'm a blur of jazzy hands and knees.
So when I think, 'this party's looking up',
it's been a while. It's late when I look up.

The Party Ends

It's been a while. It's late when I look up.
The fig and caramel mousse is going off.
The bridesmaids all look bloodshot. You've gone off
with some athletic groomsman. I look up
to drink the moony dusk. I should look up
the schedule for the bus—get going. Off
beyond the trees, the stars are going off
like sparklers. There's a woman looking up
to watch me dance out one last running man.
I'm mostly out of plans, so when she asks
I do not say I'm looking for a girl
who's run away with yet another man.
I merely smile askew, as if to ask:
You think that I'm good-looking for a girl?

Deadly Sevenlings

Wrath

Fat Bat sucks all the honey from my tea,
wraps his gamey wings around my face
and squeezes 'til the world is leather-red.

Fuck you. I'll smash my mug against the wall,
wishing my rooibos into blood. I'll chitter
a bat-nose song: *You stink. I hope you die.*

Bat scratches me; I'll rip my claws through you.

Lust

So girls don't want you. What am I,
your dog? Your looking glass? I know:
your robot psychotherapist.

It makes me hate you. I could shove
your back against those crates and bite
your lips until you begged for more.

I can slant-rhyme 'hate' with 'want'.

Gluttony

Bring me Twinkies slick in plastic,
six-pack soda, jumbo prawns.
Swaddle 'em in bacon. Fry 'em.

Let the otters choke on plastic,
oil-slicked and starved for prawns.
Piglets bleed in cages? Let 'em.

Screw your diet; it's my body.

Envy

How the hell are you a professor
with your cashmere scarves and your schoolboy French
and your head full of cottage cheese?

I'm an adjunct with a broken space heater
and perfect German. At least my brainpan
contains a wheel of brie.

Who did you blow, pretty boy? What's his number?

Sloth

I can't mop the floor. I'm busy.
I'm too tired to write.
It's too late to call my mother.

Now I've scrubbed my eyes with gravel,
drawn my hamstrings tight,
squeezed my lungs out circling on my

stationary bike.

Vanity

Here's my sister, thin as a mink on Facebook:
string bikini, doctor fiancé, highlights.
Honestly, I couldn't be jealous. I've got

curves like a mofo,
ringlets, and I look
gorgeous in corsets.

First I'll hit the gym; then I'll get my hair done.

Avarice

Why do these people expect me to pay
for their libraries, lunches, birth control?
Why can't they shut their legs, mouths, minds?

I've eaten the social contract.
I am the self-causing first cause.
I mix my labour with the infinite

and the infinite is mine.

Toothfish

Secret Sideshow

He's slight and matte as any old fish—
no swirly fins, no flashy scales—
but he's got tricks. He'll vanish goldfish
and sever tetras tip-from-tail.
His teeth would rouse a fanfare somewhere
(Woods Hole, perhaps?) but at the funfair
he floats unmarked, a minor prize
for ping-pong ball, his garnet eyes
offset by eighty-seven eyeteeth.
Here comes Gretchen, six, to press
her luck. She chucks the ball, and yes!
It splashes down on this awry-teethed
demon in a plastic dome.
She grabs the bag and brings him home.

Their Burgeoning Friendship

She grabs her schoolbag, brings him homework
(which he eats), and plays him Liszt,
explaining keenly—'listen, Fish'—
how hammers, keys and metronomes work.
He could bust through glass, through bands of
stainless steel and bite her hands off,
but when Gretchen reaches in
to scritch his fins, he purrs and grins.
They share bag lunches, Twixes, Twizzlers,
invent code names. Their secret call's
a theme from the *Mephisto Waltz*
conveyed in chirrups, burps and twitters.
She sprouts up tall and tan. He glows
pale green at night. She grows. He grows.

Sabotage

At night, he grows, the pale green glowworm
of the sea, the mutant bass
from Mars. His bulk abrades the glass
and when he shifts, the shockwaves flow from
tank to table, rise and ripple
'til the beams and floorboards wiggle.
Her mother begs her: *please forget*
your fish. Adopt some normal pet:
a bonsai tree? a snail? a puppy?
Her father, more proactive, hires
a mobster who, with sheaves and wires,
slyly garottes the goofed-up guppy.
He claims the fish has gone to romp
the hills. He throws it in the swamp.

He'll Be Back

He's in a swamp. A hellish throat-ache
burns our hero gill to gill,
and fury stabs him like a hot stake.
He'll shish-kebab them on his grill
for what they've done. They stole his Gretchen,
gouged his throat, but soon . . . his fish-grin
halves a hapless crocodile.
He veers and steers the muddy mile
toward the river—blackish, brackish,
lined with bracken fern. His jaw
is tough enough to shiver through
a human shin. He's feeling peckish.
The turbid water masks his glow.
He snarls and turns toward Tokyo.

Recovery

Gretchen's turned out okey-dokey,
says her dad. Her fishy phase
is finished. Now she studies ocean
archaeology. She'll raise
a wreck next year, complete her thesis.
Tough girl. She's picking up the pieces
of some ancient Grecian vase.
Staring at the shards, she says
nothing. There's a black glaze monster
gazing from the shattered clay
with one red eye. Far off, the sea
cries out. Her heartbeat roars an answer.
She'll find him if she has to sink
a hundred miles in the drink.

He's Sick of Being Back

He's tired. He's drunk the blood of hundreds,
left a trail of empty hulls
from port to port. The ships he's plundered
open their entrails to the gulls.
So many dead, and still no mobsters.
He's through with men. He'll switch to lobsters,
become a chef and stuff his days
with lobscouse, bisque, and bouillabaisse.
His skin still stings with steel, still itches
where fragmentary fishhooks hack
the heavy leather of his back,
but now he's done. Goodbye, cruel scratches!
Goodbye harpoons! Goodbye police!
Hello the eastern coast of Greece!

Shipwreck

Hello to Greece! The eastern coastline
waves and winks at Gretchen's ship
through gouts of rain. Stone cliffs rise ghostlike
from the storm. She bobs and dips
and whacks a rock. The hull rips open.
The sea's a Scylla: gaping, gulping
hunks of crew. It swings and knocks
our heroine onto the rocks.
While Scylla barks, she shakes and chatters
but hangs on tight. Her grip is sharp
to match the rocks. She starts to slip
when something capers through the breakers—
a shape that chitters . . . is that . . . Liszt?—
more great and green than any fish.

Epilogue

He's just the same, but bigger, greener.
She rubs his back. At last they're home.
Their pub is growing. Critics gloat:

those sumptuous roasts that fill your throat,
oaky, smoky; karaoke
Friday nights; a hundred drinks!

just off the eastern coast of Greece.

Cryptid Riddles

A Warning from the Park Ranger

Broad-nose, fluff-head clamberer. Double-thumber.
Peaceful face. A-doze in a breezy gumtop.
Watch: you'll never notice his spotted bum drop.
Camera cocked, you'll stride through the Queensland summer,

snap the deep-dish ears and the fuzzy top-hair,
click your tongue, yell 'Cuddle-ums! Come to poppa!'
Wait: don't turn your back on your back; you'll cop a

ravenous drop bear.

Lonely Hearts Ad

Sister of Diprotodon, Palorchestes.
Lurks in creeks and slavers in rivers. Seeking
tall, dark, juicy prey. Almond eyes and bee-sting
kisses. Beautiful beastie. Let's be besties.

Let's go down to the billabong, watch the sun skip,
tango to the boom of the lonesome bittern.
If you fancy the thrill of being bitten,

                                        reply to 'Bunyip'.

College Life

Who ate all the fish fingers? Bill, your roommate
blames some otter-beaver thing from New Zealand.
Look, it ate your microwave meatloaf meal and
goldfish crackers. Honestly, Bill? Fuck *you*, mate.

Christ, you need a wine cooler. What the heck, eh?
Crack the fridge. It stares at you: flat-tailed, freaky,
flipper-deep in cheesecake. You've caught a cheeky

young waitoreke.

How to Drop 12 Inches in 1 Week!

Lose ten kilos! Flatten your belly! Try it
now and get half off your tremendous torso!
Like the fig-and-water plan, only more so!
Dreamtime only! Secret is: *you're* the diet.

(Warning: Something toothless may nab and gnaw you.
May cause weakness, sucker sores, facial swelling,
bright red skin.) Celebrity chefs are yelling:

'Yara ma yha who!'

Dingo Complains About the Australian Music Scene

Sulphur-crested cockatoos? Ugh, what poseurs.
They're no punks. And emus? The lamest, hottest
faux-fur mess since kiwis. The rats on Rottnest?
Phoney quokkas. (Wannabe pointy-nosers.)

But the worst? Those times when a hipster-striper
fakes his own extinction. (Besides, no cat has
pouches.) Please quit flapping your jaw, you fat

Tasmanian tiger.

Mysterious Outback Figure

Who's that handsome outlaw? No, not Ned Kelly.
See? No armour. (Goodness! No clothes whatever!)
Feet on backwards. Not very brave, but clever.
Long, sharp nails. Thick beard, and a hairy belly.

When the sheriff threatens—Sha-zam! Ker-pow-y!
Whiz!—our hero's off with his red beard streaming,
sprinting in the other direction, screaming.

There goes the yowie!

Banjo

Word went round the village: the colt from Nessie
bolted up the creek, so we grabbed our paddles,
decked our serpents out in their Sunday saddles,
galloped to the waterfall. Things got messy

when the colt slipped off at a breakneck slither
up the Snowy Rapids. His sidelong, random
zigzag beat us frothy—all but the Man From

Hawkesbury River.

Rough Times

It's not safe, the Outback. A toothy giant
hunts with howling hunger and hoards his larder
if he wants to live. Kangaroos kick harder
now that grass is scarce. Even quolls ain't pliant.

Once we roared from Wollongong west to Freo,
lords of scrub and desert. Tails curled, we'd cruise out:
badass cats who rock out with all their claws out,

Thlylacoleo.

This Poem Is Not About You

Confessional

On daytime TV, there's a woman trapped in a man's body.
Who is this man? How can she give him back his body?

When my ex came out of the closet, she lost her moustache
and glasses. The trench coat fell from her body.

The incredible human mind! It leaps a cathedral,
soars over a sonata—and stumbles on the hillocks of the body.

I love my voice, which sings out to other women.
Is that enough? Or must I also love my body?

You can't box up your sex and demand a refund. They'll call security.
Security will ask where you buried the body.

God will smite me for my lies: girl, boi, straight, queer.
I want an indulgence, but who sells them these days? Nobody.

Forget Rachael. I'd rather be Rae, or Ray:
a brass flourish that could announce anybody.

Romantic Comedies Give Me the Screaming Meemies

Don't give me the moon. I'm not scared of outer space,
but I can't face the pressure suit, or the tiny titanium space.

The heart is a bitter apple. Bruised, it scowls behind its skin.
Bitten, it puckers around the dark space.

Poor gecko! The kookaburra is all nervous cackles.
The strangler fig weeps, its spine an empty space.

I sprint by the river, stomp concrete, swallow gnats.
The treadmill offers more speed, but less space.

Bowerbird, keep your trinkets. I'll dive
for dollar coins, a cormorant in an endless blue space.

I'm ravenous for dictionaries, donuts, disco balls.
Can you handle a woman who takes up space?

Knock yourself out, Rachael. Fill the page with chatter.
The challenge
                    is the use
                              of white space.

My Enemy

grabbed my wrists and poured sticky stuff over my mind.
Bruises wash out; there is no scrub brush for the mind.

My only souvenir is the acid scent of ants.
Were they crawling up my arm, or up my mind?

Our friends encircle him, beating their wings and cooing.
I tiptoe past. They shriek: *Have you lost your mind?*

Don't eat the fruit! He dips the peaches in antifreeze,
stuffs nails into the plums. The pomegranate seeds are mined.

Embrace me and I'll bristle. Stroke my back; I'll jangle like an alarm.
No one can unsnarl them, these nerves that used to be mine.

I smile smooth as lychees, cool as iced margaritas,
but I'm nursing a fireball in my mind.

Shh, Rachael. Chill out and grab a beer. Embrace the drum circle.
No thanks. I'll keep watch from the porch, if you don't mind.

Bypass

Sax, bass, keyboard: Uncle Pete beats syncopated time.
Some idiot kicked over the drum set. It's leaking time.

In my dreams, you splutter through a lake of anaesthetic,
fingernails lilac. The nurse shoves you under for the third time.

The surgeon drums a steel melody with clamp and scalpel,
rearranges your signature from common time to cut time.

Open your heart. Squeeze out another accordion tune for me.
Open your watch. Dig between the gear teeth for extra time.

Fluorescent light sucks the juice from my uncle's face,
preserves him like a violet between evening and nighttime.

Showdown at dawn: Pete with his smoker's heart
vs. Death on rocket-powered rollerblades. Who's got
    the faster mile time?

It's me, Rachael, shouting from the sidelines. I'm waving
a white banner, hoping Superman will show up in time.

Gnostic

To sprint, first compress the world
to a point, then hurl your body at the world.

In each eye, I carry a leaky bucket
with enough mud to gild and stain the world.

The air sings a million mosquitoes,
all modes of the one dumb world.

Cheer up, love. What more could you want?
A pretty balloon? Tickets to Sea World?

Everything tastes like the same lousy pizza topping—
pineapple and onion. Who ordered this world?

Someday, I'll step out of my blankets into a cold noplace,
swallow a glass of nothing, watch the snowflakes whirl.

More wine, Rachael? Go ahead and pour. I'll dive
down the stem of my glass to some redder, better world.

Pushpin

Forget strip shows. They say the highest pleasure
is to unlace the stays of pain and pleasure.

I know the quill that pricks the sick lung,
but what species of porcupine is pleasure?

He stumbles into her bedroom, grabs for the lube,
topples a lamp. The stings we tolerate for pleasure!

I once swallowed a time-release capsule
to melt bone and vapourise pleasure.

Press your ear to a volume of Aurelius—
hear his spine vibrate with stoic pleasure—

I'll plunk myself on the verandah to gape at galahs:
mouthful of mango, pitcherful of pleasure.

Given the choice of cake, a fuck, or a book
Ray gropes for them all, muttering *my pleasure*.

The Kingdom of Ends Ain't All It's Cracked Up to Be

You miss her breath, her alto tone. What, will
your sorry heartbeat snare the tune? What will?

She offered you her Lem novels, her lipstick,
her love forever? Yeah right. In what will?

The dog's all shaky knees and funky breath.
Some Blu-tack binds him to his skin—what? Will.

The mynahs shout. If sleep won't shut them out
(or pillows, earplugs, hip-hop, gin) what will?

The last five Ks. I launch into the wall.
Hundred-watt engine with a ten-watt will.

She'll bring me lilies, plums, champagne—or else
I've just confused *what ought to* and *what will.*

I'll pin a grin on, wrench my spine upright.
'That Rae,' she'll marvel. 'What élan. What will.'

Logic Lectures

Eristic

We pad through the agora,
waving bright bottles and shouting.
Varicoloured essences, five chalkoi apiece!
An obolus buys you an entire quiddity!
Bring home a box of syllogisms
for little Barbara, Celarent, and Felapton.

For you, we will prove the most shocking of propositions:
Csteppius is the son of a dog,
Zeno is the opposite of Theon,
no one can tell a lie,
Socrates knows everything,
truth and falsehood are one.

For a handsome enough fee, you can even uncork
the stone jug of Truth
and watch the secrets pour from its mouth like olive oil.
No warrior or statesman has ever dared
grasp its neck.
Even we, keepers of the deepest and most dazzling wisdom,
are not entirely sure what's inside.

Free Logic

Last week, we learned the logic of
the gap-toothed pond, the rotting log,
the flip-foot tadpole, halfway frog,
the muddy, half-unknitted glove,
the grackle neither black nor green
but somewhere in between.

Today, it's things that don't exist.
We'll ease in slow with Santa Claus,
or Saint Bernards with purple paws.
Although the things that don't exist
peel off like paint from those that do,
they have a logic too.

A few of them are solid as
the marathon you might have run,
the ache, the way your sneakers spun
heel over heel, true love, the jazz
guitar you might have learned to pluck,
or else your winning luck.

They breed beneath the grackle-glow, where
aspen leaf and ostrich frond
knit sweaters for the gap-toothed pond.
The tadpole tail swims off to nowhere.
The wood falls off in barky bits;
the glove unknits.

Possible Dragons

for Ruth Barcan Marcus

A possible dragon has no claws,
won't use you to pumice its pointy paws,
won't crush or roast or maul you.
A possible dragon won't haul you
away to the cave where it smokes and gnaws

(or would, if it could) the saucy sirrahs
who thought they could slay it. No, thank the laws
of logic, this won't befall you.
A possible dragon,

however, can echo its corvid caws
in a voiceless voice through its toothless jaws
to coax and curse and call you.
And he will draw closer to death, who draws
a possible dragon.

Zeno's Paradoxes

for José Benardete

The tortoise ladled up silverbeet
with half a sprig of parsley:
half to save and half to eat
and we'll never reach the end.

Achilles raced me on a dare
with half a mile of gravel.
Never got more than halfway there
and he'll never reach the end.

Achilles ran another race
with a shoe half-full of blisters
and every mile he doubled his pace
and I don't know where he'll end.

I sliced a sausage very thin
with a half a half a half a half
       a half a half a sausage—
I opened up its gutsy skin,
but I couldn't find the end.

I'd like to hunt the kangaroo
with a quiver half-full of arrows
but my feather ain't got no follow-through,
so what good's the pointy end?

I promise I'll repeat this song
with a half a mind to do it,
but honesty takes far too long,
so I guess it's time to end.

Truth

A question that will bother me until I am a rheumy old philosopher, and has bothered me since I was a
  moony youth
is: What is truth?

At first, I thought that Aristotle had got it
when he said that you speak truly when, if something is the case, you say it, and if something is not the
  case, you say not-it.

But then I ran across puzzling sentences like 'This sentence is false' and puzzling pairs of sentences like
  'Sentence One: Sentence Two is false' and 'Sentence Two:
Sentence One is true.'

Or worse, 'If this sentence is true, then you'll eat your hat, feather and all', the gist
of which is that in order to avoid paradox, you have to horrify both your milliner and your
  gastroenterologist.

So then I decided I shouldn't ramble on, since
all this talk about truth was probably incoherent, and what is incoherent is nonsense.

But I can't seem to stop. Maybe if nothing else will help me, this'll. It
is something Frank Ramsey said: what you can't say, you can't say, and you sure as hell can't whistle it.

The Phenomenal Paint Emporium

Stroll into the lobby,
where sample chips shimmer with pigments
that exist only in the mind.
Press a swatch of phosphene green against your eyeball;
stare at the impossible pink 'til you pass out.

When you come to,
gaze at our stains and glazes:
visual purple to blackout black.
Enjoy a double serve of the two-for-one cross-eyed special,
or sprinkle the force-and-vivacity blend over one of your fantasies
to watch it bloom into florid memory.

Grab a complimentary plastic spoon in Aisle Six
and dip into a tub of burnt tongue, hunger sauce,
last peach before winter.
In Aisle Seven, you can huff
the all-natural essence of puppy,
the smoke of birch bark burning.
Suck down a long drag of durian
seasoned with superhighway skunk.

Ah. Not many people inquire about the basement.
Duck through the low doorway
and grope your way down the stairs.
Pull the chain overhead to illuminate
the buckets
with no labels.
Each comes with its own utensil:

A fine point for bee stings,
a broad wire brush for poison ivy.
Stipple pins and needles over your sleeping foot.
Carve out a jumbo scoop of ice cream headache.

That one in the back?
Oh, I wouldn't dip my thumb in there if I were you.

Waiting for David K. Lewis

Since the day was starting to stink like old cheese,
Billy and I put it through the automatic slicer
and ate it before it could rot.
We're serving seconds on crackers.
You're still not here.

Who cares if your skull is packed with sprockets
and your pockets laden with model trains?
Though you always turn up three minutes early,
all snorts and stares, a question mark tangled in your beard,
we know you belong with us
in Wagga Wagga.

Come, shuffle into the dusty tea room,
where all of us—
Steffi, Biggles, Armo, the broad-eared dormouse,
even Bruce the cat
who purrs reflected heat at the teapot
and meows poetry in another possible world—
await you.

Hedges loom:
has the callistemon come to devour us?
Come, scrape your blazing blade of negation through the
    dialetheist thicket.

You will find us waiting by the billabong
with Billy boiling.
The bikkies taste like Marmite,
but they're made from pure *je ne sais quoi*.
If we sing loud enough, will you hear?

Bruce has caught an Indonesian gecko;
his pointed teeth show beneath its skin.
I am nibbling the last half-minute.

Pointy Little Stones

Classic Rock

Cocaine, Golden Brown, Needle and the Damage Done.
Dad swaddles the notes
in a voice too deep for his chest,
cradles the Melody Maker in his skinny arms.

Lou Reed's riff
runs slow then fast then slow.
Pause.
I found Uncle Mitch in his office, says Dad,
swatting flies that weren't there.
We haven't seen Uncle Mitch since he got fired
and divorced Aunt Linda.
I try to look Dad in the eye,
but he starts in again with
I guess that I just don't know.

Outside the window,
a four-point buck stares at us through the snow.
I shout at Boomer, who won't quit barking,
but Dad doesn't even glance up from his sheet music.
He can carry a tune through any kind of noise.

Burning

The human body is a torch
you mustn't touch.

When you step forward to embrace your friend,
he draws back
from your ruddy breasts with their white-hot tips.
He is afraid of you
singeing his groin, or smudging him
with a smut that won't rub out.

But you only want to press torch against torch
until the orange edge of the flame dissolves
and a single body
wraps two blue ghosts in its smoky arms.

Sunbathers at the Gold Coast

The sun melts over Currumbin,
slops invisible ink
in droplets thick as butter
over the backs of surfers
and gold-hipped basking girls.

Their skin squints to decipher
the encrypted notes that Apollo
tucks between muscle-knit shoulders,
slips down shirts, behind ears,
weaves through the gaps of toes.

Sometimes the ink uncurls
to a blue-black blotch, a name
that rewrites itself past the skin,
scrawls through liver and bone
until the pen runs out.

Wooing Entropy

Here with a Loaf of Bread beneath the Bough,
A Flask of Wine, a Book of Verse – and Thou
Beside me singing in the Wilderness –
And Wilderness is Paradise enow.
— Omar Khayyam (*Edward Fitzgerald*)

A piece of mandel bread, a glass of wine,
a book of verse, another glass of wine,
and Thou, I guess. (Not really. Truth be told,
it's all for me, this jeroboam of wine.)

Last month, you stayed to watch the night unfold;
December glazed my windows just as cold.
My ankles ached. The knuckle of the bread
clenched stiff inside its velvet glove of mould.

How many drinks until the tongue falls dead
athwart the throat, or crumbles in the head?
How many joints until the mind is gone?
Not few enough, but like Fitzgerald said,

the caravan draws onward toward the dawn.
The poet writes, and having writ, moves on.

How Much is Not Enough?

You need something to clutch at night, but I've got
only gristle and bone. You stroke my shoulder;
I imagine the blade will put your eye out,
shimmy with sharpness,
puncture your liver,
offer you tetanus.

I'm all talons and sabre teeth, and you need
bunny fur. When you pet me, you imagine
I'm the sweater your mother knit, your fawn-eyed
marabou princess,
nothing but magic,
nothing but kisses.

You need something to clutch at night, and I've got
nothing. Grit. Ashes.

Third Gender Roles

I'm sick of being the girl.
How bout I be the flugel horn,
     or the popcorn-maker,
         or the giraffe?

Yeah, how 'bout the giraffe?
I could gallop like flowing water,
     shove my phyllophagous snout into the treetops,
      snort a hot wind,

weave my tongue up my nose.
No manners. No make-up.
     I would shit on the vacuum cleaner.
      If I didn't like somebody,

I would kick them.
While we're at it,
     you can be the tiny top hat.

You can pass Go.
I can brush your nap until it's smooth as bearskin.
     We'll be the envy of goth girls everywhere.

Together, we'll be
a giraffe in a tiny top hat.
     Let's do it. Let's be anything
        except the boy and (God forbid)
      the girl.

Notes

'Mud' Karo syrup is a brand of corn syrup sold in the US, where corn is cheaper than sugarcane. Used in soap bubbles, fondant, and pecan pie.

'Raspberries' The treble leaf is a distinctive feature of poison ivy, an American plant with three-part leaves, it causes an allergic rash on contact.

'Money for nothing' The title of a Dire Straits song.
> *You get your money for nothing*
> *and your chicks for free.*

Logic Lectures These poems were inspired by my love of philosophy. If you find them inspiring, you can learn more by browsing the *Stanford Encyclopedia of Philosophy* (http://stanford.library.usyd.edu.au/) or the *Internet Encyclopedia of Philosophy* (http://www.iep.utm.edu/), both free, not-for-profit websites run by professional philosophers.

'Eristic' Plato and Aristotle's term for frivolous rhetoric (probably aimed at the Megarian school, which emphasised verbal skill and adversarial methods). For a good discussion of the history of logic, starting with ancient Greece, I recommend William and Matha Kneale's *The Development of Logic* (Clarendon Press, Oxford, 1984).

— An obolus was an ancient Athenian coin worth eight chalkoi. One obolus would buy three litres of wine, a day's rented slave labor, or a trip to the underworld on Charon's ferry.

— Syllogisms are formal arguments the way Aristotle intended, with two premises and a conclusion. Premises and conclusions come in four flavours: *A* for universal and positive ('all terriers chase rats'), *E* for universal and negative ('no terriers write poetry'), *I* for particular and positive ('some poets are terrors'), and *O* for particular and negative ('some taro roots are not purple'). Syllogisms are classified according to the flavours of their premises and conclusions. So an *AAA* syllogism (nicknamed 'Barbara') has two positive universal positive premises and a universal conclusion; e.g., 'all men are mortal; Socrates is a man; therefore, Socrates is mortal.'

'Free Logic' Classical logic (used by philosophers, mathematicians, and computer programmers) assumes that everything with a name exists. Introduce the wrong name into a conversation, and you could end up proving the existence of God, Superman, the last unicorn, or the square circle. With free logic, you can expand your conversational repertoire and avoid the awkward crowding. But even free logic doesn't settle what to say about things at the fuzzy border between existence and non-existence: nearly dry ponds; logs rotting into soil; half-unknitted gloves. For those, philosophers have logics of vagueness: supervaluationism and fuzzy logic.

'Possible Dragons' Dragons don't exist, but might have. Does this mean there are possible dragons – sofas, sets, or statues that might have been dragons? Ruth Barcan Marcus was the first logician to rigorously pose the question ('A Functional Calculus of First Order Based on Strict Implication', *Journal of Symbolic Logic* 11: 1–16).

'Zeno's Paradoxes' Zeno of Elea (5th century BCE) is known for his arguments that motion is impossible. In the Paradox of Achilles, a plodding tortoise races the warrior Achilles with a pitifully small head start. Zeno claims that Achilles can never ovetrake the tortoise. Achilles would need to cover first half the distance to the tortoise, then half the remaining distance, then half the distance left over ... The most wildly entertaining discussion of Zeno's paradoxes is Jose Benardete's book *Infinity: An Essay In Metaphysics* (Clarendon Press, Oxford, 1964). The *Stanford Encyclopedia* and *Internet Encyclopedia* entries are respectable, though less filled with madcap glee. Lewis Carroll's widely anthologised essay 'What the Tortoise Said to Achilles' addresses a related logical puzzle.

'The Phenomenal Paint Emporium' The concept of mental paint comes from Gilbert Harman: 'Imagining or picturing a unicorn is usefully compared with a painting of a unicorn' ('The Intrinsic Quality of Experience', *Philosophical Perspectives* 1980, 4: 31–52). Harman believes that mental paint is invisible, so that you can't see your imaginings any more than a canvas sees paint. Ned Block disagrees: there are mental oils 'like the oil in oil based paint' with their own colours, textures, and flavours. ('Mental Paint and Mental Latex', in *Reflections and Replies: Essays on the Philosophy of Tyler Burge*, edited by Martin Hahn and Bjorn Ramberg, MIT Press, Massachusetts, 2003).

—The force-and-vivacity blend is loosely borrowed from David Hume's *An Enquiry Concerning Human Understanding* (http://www.davidhume.org/texts/ehu.html). 'Every one will readily allow, that there is a considerable difference between the perceptions of the mind, when a man feels the pain of excessive heat, or the pleasure of moderate warmth, and when he afterwards recalls to his memory this sensation, or anticipates it by his imagination. These faculties may mimic or copy the perceptions of the senses; but they never can entirely reach the force and vivacity of the original sentiment.'

'Waiting for David K. Lewis' David Kellogg Lewis (1941–2001) is most famous for arguing that everything possible is true in some world, so that there are worlds containing talking donkeys, particles faster than light, and counterparts of Hitler who win World War II (*On the Plurality of Worlds*, Blackwell Publishers, Oxford, 1986). But he wrote about many other topics, including logic, language, mind, and ethics. He even touched on Australian poetry ('Ern Malley's Namesake', 1995, *Quadrant* 39: 14–15).

'Classic Rock' The songs (with sample lyrics) are:

> 'Cocaine' by Eric Clapton:
> *She don't lie, she don't lie she don't lie,*
> *cocaine*

> 'Golden Brown' by the Stranglers:
> *Golden brown, texture like sun . . .*
> *Never a frown with golden brown*

> 'The needle and the damage done' by Neil Young:
> *I see the needle and the damage done,*
> *a little part of it in everyone*

'Heroin' by Lou Reed:
when I'm rushing on my run
and I feel just like Jesus' son
and I guess I just don't know

Acknowledgements

A version of 'Singularity' appeared in issue #38 of *Rattle* (1 December, 2012).

Thanks to Varuna House for housing me, feeding me, and allowing me access to Eleanor Dark's studio for a week while I worked on this book. Thanks to Jeanne Gauthier, Michelle Arneson, and Bradshaw Stanley for detailed comments on earlier drafts of the manuscript. Thanks to my old teachers Herman Card and Brooks Haxton, for encouraging me to take up poetry and keep at it. And many thanks to everybody at The Poetry Free-For-All (http://www.everypoet.org/pffa/) for the feedback, the reality checks, and the moral support.